Getting To Know...

Nature's Children

KOALAS

Elizabeth MacLeod

Grolier

Facts in Brief

Classification of the Koala

Class: *Mammalia* (mammals)

Order: *Marsupialia* (pouch-bearing mammals)

Family: *Phascolarctidae* (koala family)

Genus: *Phascolarctos*

Species: *Phascolarctos cinerus*

World distribution. Australia.

Habitat. Eucalyptus forests.

Distinctive physical characteristics. Reddish or gray coat that is lighter on the ears and underside; long strong claws; cheek pouches to store food. The female has a stomach pouch where she carries her young during the first part of their lives.

Habits. Solitary; spends most of its time eating, sleeping, and looking for food; is most active at night, feeding and defending its territory.

Diet. The leaves of the eucalyptus tree.

This series is approved and recommended by the Federation of Ontario Naturalists.

Canadian Cataloguing in Publication Data

MacLeod, Elizabeth.
  Koalas/Elizabeth MacLeod. Cheetahs/Alia Smyth

(Getting to know—nature's children)
Issued also in French under title: Le koala ; Le guépard.
Includes indexes.
ISBN 0-7172-2606-9

1. Koalas—Juvenile literature.   2. Cheetahs—Juvenile literature.
I. Smyth, Alia.   II. Title.   III. Title: Cheetahs.   IV. Series.

QL737.M384M24 1989   j599.2   C89-093649-8

Have you ever wondered . . .

where the word *koala* comes from?   page 5

how a young koala calls for help?   page 6

who the koala's relatives are?   page 9

where koalas live?   page 10

if koalas live in dens?   page 13

whether koalas like company?   page 13

how big an adult koala is?   page 14

what a koala's tail is like?   page 14

if koalas have a good sense of smell?   page 17

what makes koalas such good climbers?   page 18

where the koala spends most of its life?   page 21

if koalas can swim?   page 22

if koalas are picky eaters?   page 26

how much a koala eats?   page 26

what koalas smell like?   page 29

where koalas usually sleep?   page 30

how koalas beat the heat?   page 33

what kind of noises koalas make?   page 34

if male koalas help raise the babies?   page 37

what a newborn koala looks like?   page 38

how long a baby stays in its mother's pouch?   page 41

how young koalas get around?   page 42

when young koalas set out on their own?   page 45

Words To Know   page 47

Index   page 48

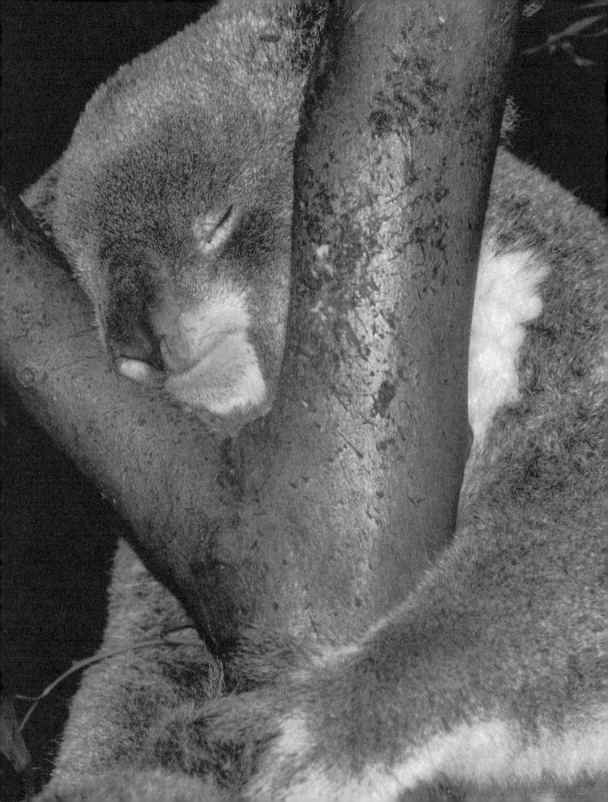

High up in a tall tree, a fluffy gray ball sits wedged in a fork of the branches. Slowly the ball begins to uncurl and soon you can see a sleepy-looking face and four furry legs. It's a koala waking up and it's already reaching for a branch of eucalyptus leaves to munch.

Koala is an Australian aboriginal word that means "animal that does not drink." It's true that koalas rarely drink—they get all the water they need from the juicy eucalyptus leaves they eat. And eating eucalyptus leaves is one of a koala's favorite things to do.

If you would like to find out more about koalas and how they live, just turn the page.

Cuddly Cubs

A young koala usually rides on its mom's back as she moves around the treetops in search of food. Clinging to her fur, the little one feels safe and protected. It will be several months before the cub is brave enough to let go and start exploring the world by itself.

If the cub should get lost or need help, it will cry until its mother comes to the rescue. People who have heard a young koala's distress call say it sounds almost exactly like the cry of a human baby!

Hitching a ride!

Animals with Pouches

Many people call koalas "koala bears" but they aren't bears at all. Koalas belong to a group of animals called marsupials. These animals give birth to young that are so tiny the mother has to shelter them in a pouch for several months while they finish developing. Kangaroos, wallabies and opossums are other marsupials.

Most scientists think that the koala's closest relative is the wombat, a stout, large-nosed animal that lives on the ground. Even though koalas live in trees, they have many things in common with wombats, including downward-facing pouches. You might think that the koala baby would fall out of a pouch that opens downward, but the cub is safe and snug inside. Later you'll see why this is the perfect pocket for a koala.

The shy wombat leaves its underground burrow at night to feed on grass, bark and roots.

Home Down Under

Australia is the only place to find koalas in the wild. They once lived in many places on that island continent, but now they can only be found along its east coast. The koalas that live to the north where the climate is warm have reddish fur coats that are short and light. Southern koalas have dark gray fur and are larger than their northern cousins. And since these southern koalas face colder weather, their fur is longer and thicker.

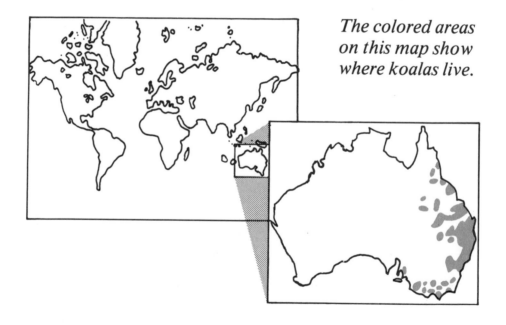

The colored areas on this map show where koalas live.

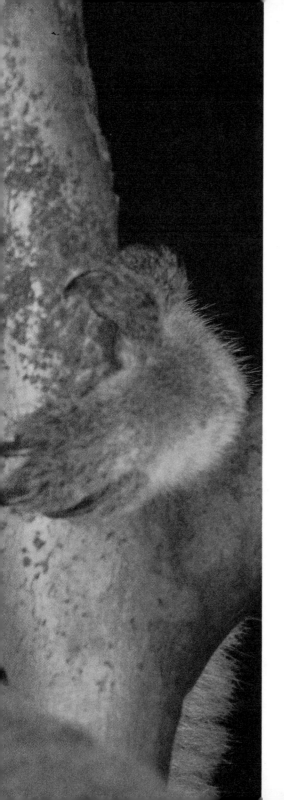

Treetop Territory

Although a koala does have a territory it calls home, it does not make a den or nest and it doesn't even claim a particular tree as its own. But koalas are not very sociable. A male koala may share a territory with two or three females as well as some younger males, but they all do their best to avoid one another. In fact, two koalas rarely sleep or even feed in the same tree unless it is very big. The koala that is already in the tree will growl a warning to any new arrival to "Keep moving!"

Some koalas may stick together, but usually they ignore each other unless it's mating season.

Koalas Up Close

Most people find koalas very appealing. Their sleepy, blinking eyes make them look wise, and their fluffy fur makes you want to pick them up and cuddle them.

An adult koala is about the size of a large bulldog. A male may weigh up to 14 kilograms (30 pounds), about as much as an average three-year-old child. Females are smaller and weigh less than males.

The fur on a koala's stomach and the long fur on its ears tend to be a lighter color than the rest of its fur. There are also usually white patches on its rump. This dappled fur probably helps camouflage the koala. An animal looking up from below would find it hard to see the koala against the shadows of the leaves. A koala has only a short, stumpy tail so there is nothing to get in the way when it sits in a tree.

Koalas have very strong arm and shoulder muscles, ideal for climbing and hanging on to trees.

Super Sniffer

Koalas are born with a good sense of smell, and they never lose it. Adults can easily sniff out the nearest food tree or tell how many koalas are nearby. They also have a keen sense of hearing because their large ears help focus sound.

Koalas are most active at night, especially just after sunset. Like most nocturnal animals, they don't rely very much on their eyesight. In fact, compared to other creatures of the night, their eyes are very small.

A nose for what's happening.

Front paw

Back paw

Handy Paws

A koala has multi-purpose paws. The fingers of its front paws are separated into two groups, with the first two fingers divided from the other three. This makes these paws especially good for grasping and climbing.

On the koala's back feet, the first toe sticks out in much the same way as your thumb. Like you, the koala uses its "thumb" to hold on to things. It uses its second and third toes, which are joined together, to comb its fur. The fourth and fifth toes have strong claws and are good for climbing.

Both the front and back paws have thick rough pads on the bottom. These help the koala grip branches and tree trunks as it moves about. They also act as cushions when it leaps from branch to branch. As well, the koala's long, strong claws not only help it to hold on when climbing, but also help it defend itself against enemies such as wild dogs, large birds and giant lizards.

Mother koala must hold on tight with the extra weight on her back.

18

Getting Around in the Trees

With its incredible sense of balance, a koala is completely at home eating, sleeping and moving about high in the trees. When it wants to move to a new tree, the koala climbs along a branch until it bends and touches the branches of the next tree. Then the koala climbs along this "bridge" into the new tree and promptly starts munching.

A koala is a speedy climber. Clasping the tree trunk with its front claws, it quickly pulls up its hind legs to its front paws. All this happens so fast, it looks as if the koala is leaping up the tree.

Getting Around Below

When a koala runs out of nearby trees to climb, it must come down to the ground. Slowly and carefully it backs down the tree. Once it hits the ground, it quickly bounds over to the nearest feeding tree and leaps to safety.

Believe it or not, a koala is also a strong swimmer. It looks very clumsy as it slowly paddles through the water, with just a little of its head showing. Once it reaches land, it shakes itself so hard to dry off that its ears slap against its head!

Heading for cover!

Look Out!

If you ever visit Australia, keep your eyes open for this sign by the roadside. Koalas don't like moving through thick bushes and grasses so they'll often walk on roads. They don't seem to be at all disturbed by cars and will even cause traffic jams by sitting down in the middle of the road! Usually no one wants to try to move a koala since it can put up quite a fight with its strong, sharp claws. Instead, traffic waits until the koala has finished resting.

Koalas may live up to 20 years in the wild.

Leafy Lunch

A koala eats almost nothing but the leaves of eucalyptus trees. And not just any eucalyptus tree. This little animal is a very picky eater and will munch on only certain leaves of certain trees.

Although most other animals find eucalyptus leaves bad tasting and can't digest them, a koala has a special stomach that lets it eat these leaves. But it must be careful. Why? The younger leaves contain a deadly poison. Koalas quickly learn to eat only the older leaves that have lost most of the poison.

Powerful jaw muscles and strong biting and grinding teeth help the koala eat up to one kilogram (2 pounds) of eucalyptus leaves each day. This furry muncher uses pouches in its cheeks to store food as it chews.

There is not much nutritional value in eucalyptus leaves, that's why koalas must eat so many.

Coughdrop Coat

The oily eucalyptus leaves provide koalas with more than just the food and water they need. The strong-smelling oils in the leaves give koalas their characteristic coughdrop smell. It's a very strong odor and can be rather unpleasant, but it keeps fleas and parasites out of the koala's beautiful, soft fur.

Is there anything cuter?

Z-z-z-z-z-z-z

Koalas sleep up to 18 hours each day, usually waking up only to eat. What a life!

Most koalas like to sleep high in the trees, and they usually don't bother to try and hide from enemies. They just nestle into the fork of a tree or wrap themselves around a branch with their paws folded together or hanging down loosely. Or a koala may sleep resting on the pad of thickened skin at the base of its back. It may lean its head against a branch to be more secure, but doesn't always.

In fact, koalas can fall asleep in almost any position. Sometimes they even fall asleep in the middle of eating! You can see leaves hanging out of their mouths as they doze. Or a baby may fall asleep with its little head hanging out of its mother's pouch.

Falling asleep on the job.

Beat the Heat

Summer in Australia can be extremely hot, and the koala can find its thick fur coat very uncomfortable. If the day really warms up, a koala may move from the eucalyptus tree where it spent the night feeding to a leafier tree that provides more shade. There it sprawls along the branch in a position that will shade it from the sun. When it is really hot, the koala eats much less and only moves to find a cooler spot.

Noisy Neighbors

Koalas are quiet most of the day, but when night falls they can be very noisy. Males are especially loud and will warn other males away from their trees with harsh grating noises that sound like a handsaw going through wood. During the mating season, a male tries to attract females to him by using low roars, bellows and mews. He may also use a cry that sounds a bit like a sneeze and another that sounds like loud ticking. A female will roar and croon in response until the two find each other.

Sounding off.

Summer Romance

Mating season for koalas is spring and summer, which in Australia is September to February. Each male patrols his territory carefully, looking for females. To mark the boundaries of his territory, the male rubs a gland on his chest against the trees. This scent marker warns other males to keep away. Fights often break out between the males at this time and can be quite vicious.

Koalas only stay together to mate. When the baby is born a little over a month later, the female raises it on her own.

Treetop mates.

Incredible Journey

Mother koalas usually give birth to only one cub every other year. Before the baby is born, mom carefully cleans out her pouch. The pouch is tough and elastic. Once it is thoroughly clean, the mother koala licks a trail to her pouch for her baby to follow.

When the baby is born, it is about the size and shape of a small jellybean. It is pink, hairless and glistening wet. The baby's back legs are just bumps, but its front paws and arms are well developed. It will need them to help pull itself to its mother's pouch. The baby almost looks like it is swimming through the fur on its mother's belly.

Although the tiny traveler is blind and deaf, instinct helps it find the pouch and it climbs in. There, the baby fastens its mouth to a nipple so it can feed on its mother's rich milk. The baby's mouth isn't developed enough to hang on, but the end of the nipple enlarges and fits into ridges in the tiny mouth so it can't let go.

This young koala must return regularly to its mother's pouch.

In the Pouch

The baby koala stays in its mother's pouch for about six months. During that time, its eyes open and it grows fur. Its back legs also develop, and during the last few weeks it spends in the pouch it kicks almost continually. Poor mom!

The little koala must learn to eat eucalyptus leaves. At first its mother feeds it pre-digested leaves. She provides this food from an opening just below her tail. That's why a downward-facing pocket is perfect for a koala. It makes it easy for the baby to reach its food supply.

Hang on tight!

Hello, World

When the baby first comes out of its mother's pouch, the world looks pretty frightening and it often climbs back in for shelter. That's tough on mom, especially when she's climbing. She must keep her stomach clear of any stubs on the tree that might hurt the baby in her pouch. However, things get easier once the baby moves onto its mom's back and rides around clasping her tightly with its arms. Being on the mother's back is also more comfortable for the baby. Why? When mom leaps from tree to tree she lands stomach first with quite a thud!

At first the baby is too scared to let go of its mom's fur to grab and eat leaves. But soon the smell of the eucalyptus becomes irresistible and the baby begins to feed.

After about five months the mother koala begins weaning her baby off milk.

Growing Up

A koala baby stays close to its mother for a few months after leaving her pouch. Even when it gets older, it will crawl onto her back if it is lonely or tired. Soon, however, mom refuses to let it climb on board and she lets the baby know that it is time for it to start a life of its own. If the baby is male, this means it may soon have to find its own territory.

As more and more trees in Australia are cut down to make room for houses and farms, it is becoming difficult for koalas to find places to live and feed. Many people are now working hard to help preserve this lovable animal's favorite eucalyptus trees. Thanks to their efforts, koalas will be able to continue to lead their sleepy lives high in Australia's treetops.

Koalas are strict but devoted mothers.

Special Words

Camouflage Fur or feathers that are colored so that they blend into the surroundings, making the animal difficult to see.

Cub A young koala.

Den An animal home.

Eucalyptus Tall, broadleaf evergreen tree native to Australia.

Marsupial An animal, such as the koala, that spends the first part of its life in a pouch in its mother's body.

Mate To come together to produce young. Either member of an animal pair is also the other's mate.

Mating season The time of the year when animals mate.

Nocturnal Most active at night.

Territory An area that an animal or group of animals lives in and usually defends from other animals of the same kind.

INDEX

baby. *See* cub

camouflage, 14
claws, 18, 25
climbing, 18, 21
communication, 6, 13, 34
cub, 6, 9, 37, 38, 42, 45
    size, 38
    growth rate, 39

defense, 18, 25
diet, 26
distribution, 10
drinking, 5

ears, 17
enemies, 18
eyes, 17

female, 13, 14, 34, 37, 38, 41, 42, 45
fur, 10, 14, 29, 33

lifespan, 25

male, 13, 14, 34, 37
marsupial, 9
mating, 13, 34, 37
mouth, 26

nose, 17

paws, 18
pouch, 9, 38, 41, 42

relatives, 9

senses, 17
size, 14
sleeping, 30
social organization, 13
swimming, 22

tail, 14
territory, 13, 37
types of, 10

weight, 14

Cover Photo: E.R. Degginger

Photo Credits: Bill Ivy, pages 4, 8, 12, 20, 27, 30, 35, 36, 46; Four By Five Inc., pages 7, 16; John Cancalosi, pages 11, 39, 40, 43; E.R. Degginger, page 15; Erwin and Peggy Bauer, pages 19, 23; Cincinnati Zoo, page 24; Australian Picture Library (The Stock Market Inc.), page 28; Kjell B. Sandved, pages 32, 44.

Getting To Know...

Nature's Children

CHEETAHS

Alia Smyth

Grolier

Facts in Brief

Classification of the Cheetah

    Class: *Mammalia* (mammals)

    Order: *Carnivora* (meat-eaters)

    Family: *Felidae* (cat family)

    Genus: *Acinonyx*

    Species: *Acinonyx jubatus*

World distribution.   Asia and Africa.

Habitat.   Plains and lightly wooded areas.

Distinctive physical characteristics.   Spotted fur; long legs; blunt, non-retracting claws.

Habits.   Hunts by day; sneaks up on prey, then puts on an astonishing burst of speed over a short distance to make the kill; female raises her cubs alone; mates stay together for only a few days.

Diet.   Grazing animals such as gazelles and antelopes.

Canadian Cataloguing in Publication Data

MacLeod, Elizabeth.
  Koalas / Elizabeth MacLeod. Cheetahs / Alia Smyth

(Getting to know—nature's children)
Issued also in French under title: Le koala ; Le guépard.
Includes indexes.
ISBN 0-7172-2606-9

1. Koalas—Juvenile literature.   2. Cheetahs—Juvenile literature.
I. Smyth, Alia.   II. Title.   III. Title: Cheetahs.   IV. Series.

QL737.M384M24 1989   j599.2   C89-093649-8

Have you ever wondered . . .

if baby cheetahs like to play?   page 6

who a cheetah's relatives are?   page 9

what makes a cheetah different from other cats?   page 9

where cheetahs live?   page 10

how big cheetahs can grow?   page 14

why the cheetah has a spotted coat?   page 14

how fast cheetahs can run?   page 17

why a cheetah has such a long tail?   page 17

if cheetahs live alone or in groups?   page 21

how a cheetah stays clean?   page 22

if cheetahs take baths?   page 22

what cheetahs eat?   page 25

how a cheetah hunts?   page 29

how long it takes a cheetah to catch its prey?   page 30

how a cheetah finds a mate?   page 33

how many babies a mother cheetah has?   page 34

what newborn cheetahs look like?   page 34

when a cheetah cub begins to walk?   page 38

how cheetah cubs learn to hunt?   page 43

when young cheetahs are ready to leave home?   page 43

how long cheetahs live?   page 44

if a cheetah has any enemies?   page 46

Words To Know   page 47

Index   page 48

If you visit the great plains of Africa during the day, the only member of the cat family you are likely to see stalking in the grass is a lone cheetah.

At first, you might think you are looking at a leopard. Both cheetahs and leopards have tawny coats with dark round spots. So how do you tell them apart?

Cheetahs are taller and more elegant and they have much longer, more graceful legs than a leopard does. It's these long legs that make the cheetah the fastest mammal on earth.

The sleek cheetah is certainly one of the world's most beautiful cats.

What Fun!

Young cheetahs love nothing more than a good romp through the tall grasses around them. There is so much to do, and a whole world to discover! When they get tired of playing with one another, they can practice their pouncing techniques on their mother's tail, or better yet, stalk the lizards that slither through the grass.

However, they are still young, and all this exercise under the hot sun quickly tires them out. After a healthy meal of their mother's milk, they waddle over to the closest bush and collapse in the shade for a long nap. As the sun beats down and the cicadas hum, the only alert figure that remains is the mother cheetah, keeping a wary eye out for any danger to her happy, chubby brood.

Cats, Big and Small

The cat family is divided into two groups: big cats and small cats. The difference between the groups is not that they are big and small. It is that big cats can roar, but they cannot purr. And small cats? You guessed it. They can purr but they cannot roar.

The cheetah is usually considered a big cat. But because it is different from the other big cats (lions, tigers, leopards and jaguars), the cheetah has its own special branch on the family tree.

What's so different about the cheetah? Mainly that it is the only cat that cannot retract its claws. In other words, its claws are always showing, like those of a dog. This helps the cheetah grip the ground when it puts on sudden bursts of speed.

There's another difference between the cheetah and other cats. All cats have whiskers that help them sense what is in front of them in the dark. The cheetah's whiskers, however, are less developed than those of other cats because it is usually out in daylight and has little use for them.

Opposite page: *Note how much less prominent the cheetah's whiskers are than those of the domestic cat.*

Opposite page:
Climbing up on a rocky ledge gives the cheetah a good view of its surroundings.

Cheetah Territory

Scientists believe that cheetahs originated in southern Asia. A very few can still be found there and in the Middle East, but today most cheetahs live on the vast plains of Africa. There, they have plenty of room to run and they can easily keep track of their prey. At the same time, the tall grasses provide the cover they need to hunt successfully. Cheetah territory is also likely to include lightly wooded areas where the cheetahs can rest safely and keep their cubs out of harm's way.

The colored areas of this map show where cheetahs live.

The Cheetah Up Close

The cheetah is one of the smaller "big" cats. The largest weighs no more than 65 kilograms (143 pounds) and is probably not much more than a metre (3.3 feet) long from its shoulder to the root of its long tail. Females are usually slightly smaller than males.

The outstanding feature of the cheetah's appearance is, of course, its beautiful spotted coat. But beauty is not all this sleek, elegant coat has to recommend it. It also serves as excellent camouflage. Crouched in the grass or lying in the dappled sunlight under a tree, a cheetah blends in so well with its surroundings that it can hardly be seen.

The most distinctive features of the cheetah's face are the dark "tear lines" running down from its eyes along both sides of its nose. These lines help break up the outline of the cheetah's face, making it even more difficult to detect. They are also thought to keep down the sun's glare, allowing the cheetah to stare for long periods of time.

Opposite page:
The leopard too has a spotted coat, but it lacks the cheetah's distinctive "tear lines".

Fast Cat

The cheetah's streamlined body is built for speed. Its long, slender bones and extremely flexible spine enable it to make incredibly long, rapid strides. When in a full run, a cheetah could easily pass a car driving along the highway. However, the cheetah can't maintain that speed for long. After about 400 metres (1/4 mile), it gets winded.

Other features help the cheetah speed along. Its small ears, flattened close to its head, create less wind resistance during a run. And its distinctive tail, almost as long as its body, serves as a rudder during high speed chases, enabling the cheetah to change direction quickly and with minimum loss of speed.

The cheetah's long tail provides balance as it sprints.

Freeze!

You may be surprised to learn that cheetahs are almost as good at keeping still as they are at running fast. In fact, a cheetah would make a champion "frozen tag" player. If it senses danger it can easily freeze and stay totally motionless for up to 20 minutes at a time.

This trick is also very useful when the cheetah is hunting and has to wait for the right moment to attack. Most of the animals the cheetah hunts keep alert for movement to signal the presence of an enemy. Unless they catch a whiff of a cheetah's scent, they probably won't notice it, even if it is lying very close and staring them right in the eye!

Zeroing in on dinner.

Keep Your Distance

Unlike other big cats, cheetahs are not necessarily aggressive toward other members of their species. In fact, several cheetahs may have overlapping territories—or even share the same one. Males will, however, attack any strangers that venture into their territory.

Actually, cheetahs do not fight among themselves very often because they have a unique way of marking their surroundings—they spray urine to mark the paths they are taking. If other cheetahs come by within 24 hours and smell this scent, they will automatically go in the opposite direction. After a full day has passed, the original markings fade. Any newcomers will still be aware of them, but they will know that there is little danger of running into whoever left the markings.

This system allows cheetahs to share the small space available for hunting game. This is especially important during the dry season when the animals they hunt congregate around the few available waterholes.

*Opposite page:
An adult cheetah patrols its territory.*

Keeping Clean

Cats are well known for their cleanliness, and cheetahs are no exception. After they have eaten their fill, they often spend great parts of the day lying in the shade of an acacia tree grooming themselves.

Except for a mother with her babies, female cheetahs live alone and avoid one another. Males, on the other hand, are more sociable and most of them live in small groups. Just as a mother grooms her kittens, male cheetahs will help one another with those hard-to-get-at places—behind the ears, for instance. As well as keeping them clean, this social grooming helps maintain the bonds within the group.

Cheetahs do not like to get wet, but they do take dust baths. As they romp around and kick up the dust they aren't just having fun. The dust baths help rid the cheetah of annoying fleas and ticks.

Male cheetahs sometimes have a short mane along their back and the nape of their neck.

Pass the Meat, Please

Like all cats, cheetahs are carnivores, or meat-eaters. They prey on antelopes, gazelles, impalas or young wildebeests and zebras. An adult cheetah usually eats about 3 kilograms (6 1/2 pounds) of meat a day. It doesn't drink very often, though—just once every four days or so. And during the dry season, cheetahs can quite comfortably go as long as nine or ten days without water.

Unlike many animals, cheetahs are quite peaceable during their meals. They seem to feel that there is plenty of food for all and that there is no need to snarl or snap at one another.

Hunter's Eyes

The cheetah has the kind of vision it needs to help it hunt successfully. Its eyes, like yours, face forward. This helps it to judge the distance between itself and its prey. Why is this important? Since a cheetah cannot run fast for very long, it must choose its moment to attack very carefully. If it misjudged the distance it had to run, it might get tired and have to quit before making its kill.

Most of the animals the cheetah hunts have eyes on the *sides* of their head. That means they can spot predators that are sneaking up behind them. The cheetah must be extremely cautious during its approach if it is to be successful.

The cheetah's long fangs are ideal for eating meat.

Stalk-and-Chase

Most other cats set off at night, often in groups, to do their hunting. Not the cheetah. It sets off in the morning, usually by itself.

Cheetahs hunt using the stalk-and-chase method. When it spots a herd, a cheetah looks for the weakest animal, usually one that is old, sick or lame.

Crouching close to the earth, it silently creeps toward its unsuspecting prey. When it is about 30 metres (100 feet) away, it springs forward and begins the chase. Some animals try to trick the cheetah by zigzagging. But the speeding cheetah pulls up beside the fleeing animal, knocks it down and lunges for its throat.

Cheetahs hunt by sight and stealth.

A Hard-Earned Meal

A cheetah's hunt can take anywhere from one minute to several hours to complete. Only about half the hunts are successful. If the prey is healthy, fast and alert it has a good chance of escaping.

Once a cheetah has made its kill, the rest of the herd it was stalking calmly continue grazing nearby. Although they remain alert for other predators, they know that the cheetah will not attack again that day.

Meanwhile, the cheetah usually drags its victim under a bush before it begins eating in order to hide it from the vultures that will soon be circling overhead looking for a free meal.

Cheetahs rarely return to a kill. Once they have eaten their fill, they wander away, leaving the remains to the scavengers with whom they share their territory.

After a big meal the cheetah likes to take it easy.

Let's Get Acquainted

When it's time to find a mate, a female cheetah attracts males by squirting urine throughout her territory. As soon as a male discovers the scent he follows it, calling to her with yelps and chirrups. She responds and the concert continues until the two find each other. If there is a group of males, the group leader is the one to mate with the female, while the other males wait nearby.

The two stay together for a few days, playing and grooming one another. Then the male returns to his companions.

Small and Helpless

After a three-month pregnancy, the mother cheetah looks for a very dense bush or thicket. There she gives birth to her small, blind and hairless cubs. Usually there will be three of them, but there may be as few as one or as many as eight.

The cubs may begin crawling on the fourth day or so, but their eyes won't open until they are about ten days old. By this time, a mantle of blue-gray fur will have grown on their heads and backs. This thick fur will protect them from the sun and rain during the next few months.

Cheetah cubs may be born at any time of the year.

A Dangerous Time

The mother cheetah keeps her cubs hidden during the first few weeks of their life. This is a dangerous time for them. Their mother must leave them unguarded every morning when she goes off to hunt. Unlike lions, which live in large family groups, cheetahs don't have an extended family to help with babysitting.

To keep the cubs safe and to ensure that their hiding place is not discovered by any lurking predators, the mother moves them every few days.

Huddling under their mother protects these cubs not only from enemies but also from the hot sun.

Fun and Games

As the cubs grow older, it becomes more and more difficult for their mother to keep them confined and hidden. They take their first tottering steps at about three weeks. By six weeks they are eagerly exploring the world around them, chasing butterflies and pouncing on flowers blowing in the wind or anything else that moves. It's all great fun, but it is more than that. The youngsters are actually beginning to develop the skills they will need to become successful hunters.

The mother cheetah keeps a fond but watchful eye on them as they frolic. She doesn't mind them climbing over her or even nipping at her tail. But should one of them start to wander off, she immediately calls it back using either a chirping call that sounds like the cheep of a chick, or a stutter call that is rather like a pigeon's coo.

Carefree Cubs

For the first six months of their life, the cubs are fed entirely by their mother. Until they are about six weeks old, they only drink her milk. After that, she brings home meat which she often chews up for them to eat.

The mother cheetah spends all her free time with her cubs, watching over them, grooming them and playing with them. But after about six months of play-practice it is time to teach them how to hunt.

Learning the Ropes

At first the mother takes her cubs out just to watch her hunt. At this stage, they are often more of a hindrance than a help. When the action starts they forget to be quiet and often scare the prey away. But a cheetah mother is patient. For the next six months she keeps teaching them the tricks they will need to survive on their own.

By the time they are about one year old, the young cheetahs are properly trained, but they stay with their mother for another three months or so. Then she chases them away. It's time for them to begin living on their own and for her to raise a new family.

After they leave their mother, the youngsters will probably live together as a group for a few more months. The females then leave, each to live on her own, but the males often stay together, sometimes for life.

This young cheetah still has a lot to learn before it can hunt big game on its own.

Solo Stalking

Life is not easy for a young cheetah recently separated from its mother. Although the cheetah has had a fair amount of hunting practice, it is not yet very skilled. Many cheetahs starve or come very close to starving at this stage of their lives. And not only must they find and catch their prey, but also they must learn to avoid lions, leopards and humans.

With luck and experience, about one third of all cheetah cubs grow into adults.

Cheetahs may live 10 to 12 years in the wild.

Facing the Future

The cheetah has several natural enemies. Both lions and leopards have been known to make a meal of a cheetah during desperate times. And scavengers such as vultures and jackals are capable of chasing a cheetah away from its kill.

Sadly, however, it is human beings that constitute the greatest threat to the continued survival of the cheetah. Although cheetahs are an endangered species and are protected worldwide, poaching is very difficult to control. Even more serious is the disappearance of their habitat. As more and more land is taken over for farming, cheetahs, lions, leopards, and the animals they hunt are pushed back into an ever smaller range and into fierce competition for food. Even the cheetah's long legs can't help it run from this situation.

Fortunately, people are now more aware of this problem than they used to be. There is every reason to hope that the efforts being made to help these magnificent creatures in their struggle to survive will be successful.

Special Words

Camouflage Fur or feathers that are colored so that they blend into the background, making an animal hard to see.

Carnivore Literally, "meat-eater." A mammal that feeds mainly on flesh.

Cub A young cheetah.

Habitat The area or type of area in which an animal or plant naturally lives.

Mammal Any warm-blooded animal that gives birth to live young and produces milk to feed them.

Mate To come together to produce young. Also, either member of an animal pair is the other's mate.

Plains Flat unforested lands.

Poaching To hunt or fish illegally.

Predator An animal that hunts others for food.

Prey An animal hunted by another animal for food.

Stalk To follow prey stealthily and quietly.

Territory Area that an animal or group of animals lives in and often defends from other animals of the same kind.

INDEX

baby. *See* cubs
baths, 22
bones, 17

camouflage, 14
claws, 9
cubs, 10, 34, 37, 38, 39, 43

drinking, 25

ears, 17
eyes, 26

fangs, 26
feeding, 25, 30
fur, 34

grooming, 22

hunting, 18, 29, 30, 37, 44

jaguar, 9

legs, 5
leopard, 5, 9, 14, 44, 46

lion, 9, 44, 46

mane, 22
mating, 33

nose, 14

pregnancy, 34
prey, 25
purring, 9

roaring, 9

speed, 17
spine, 17
spots, 5, 14

tail, 14, 17
tear lines, 14
tiger, 9

vision, 26

whiskers, 9

Cover Photo: Bill Ivy

Photo Credits: Bill Ivy, pages 4, 8, 20, 31; Boyd Norton, pages 7, 11, 12-13, 20, 23, 35, 45; Hans Ruysenaar (Canapress), page 15; G. Ziesler (Peter Arnold Inc./Hot Shots), page 16; Erwin and Peggy Bauer, page 19; New York Zoological Soceity, page 24; Cincinnati Zoo, page 27; Breck P. Kent, page 28; Brian Beck (StockMarket Inc.), page 32; Metro Toronto Zoo, page 36; Columbus Zoo, page 40-41; Selwyn Powers (Sandved and Coleman), page 42.